THE
SQUAW VALLEY
REVIEW 2011

AN ANTHOLOGY OF POEMS BY
MEMBERS OF THE SQUAW VALLEY
COMMUNITY OF WRITERS 2011

D1015992

COMMUNITY OF WRITERS

Squaw Valley, CA

THE SQUAW VALLEY REVIEW

Editor: Marcelo Hernandez Castillo

Editorial Team: Brent Calderwood
Amy Hoffmann
Leah Kaminski
Terry Lowe
Sally McNall
Brent Schaeffer
Nicole Sealey
Erica Zora Wrightson

Editorial Advisor: Robert Hass

Cover Photograph: Brett Hall Jones
Cover Design: Amy Hoffmann
Book Typography: Brent Calderwood

THE SQUAW VALLEY REVIEW

TORY ADKISSON

REFRAIN

About the swan: he'll dip his head
until it's wet with ink. Slick neck

& loose string of pearls. About the
swan: he'll be pleased if his bull-bill

parts your legs neatly. A little leg
is all he wants, & he wants what he

can't have: the little bruise on your
calf. About the swan: you'll be fine

if you remain still when he enters you,
swinging wide the door of your body,

brutal with light, his voice the size
of an olive, an octave between rain & snow.

Your tongue is adhesive. He'll never
quiet unless you seal his trap shut

& gnash your teeth like sabers. He'll
enjoy, & see the foreplay, in all this.

About the swan: he'll smell your fear
& eagerness to be eaten whole, to be

pitted. He'll dirty the stars shooting
through your moonstruck hair. About

the swan: he will not be satisfied after
plumbing you & pulling out all the dead

leaves in your chest, the glass eggs sterile
in your belly. He'll happily lap the tears

cloistered in your lashes & think only
of ways to open your tightly-fastened eyes.

WHAT EVE TOOK

From you, she stole moments, brief
filigree, before you knew the word

for *pleasure*, meaning the patina growing
large on your flesh. Later, she took

an x-acto knife to your arm, unraveling
your arteries like bubble wrap
meant to embrace something sacred

that was never packaged, perhaps
never even built. She saw herself as missing

jigsaw piece, & more—she felt within herself
the absence of ivory & glass. You acted as though
you never felt that abandonment, that every element

of your body fell into place
as it might, or ought to have,
at the seminal moments of construction.

Humanity was embroidered by clouds
once, before a higher power
tried & failed to chew off the rough edges.

This was before our cardinal sin, before
autumn's denigration of your union

with her & the fruit's glossy
skin stuck in your jaw. Just one bite

tickled her hair, made your insides quiver
& loin leaf stand erect. When she found

her voice, she pointed
a thumb & forefinger beneath your jaw

like a gun. After this, she'd lay awake
every night, imagining you falling into a snake's nest,
their elastic bodies snapping & snapping

back like rubber bands. How could she not
resent your oblivious, looming presence?

Life was no better after exile, but
the trepanation of paradise was

close to perfect. The erasure of her singular innocence
from your brute body, her memories

implausible & faded like the paintings
in a cave your hands

made of their own accord—
& as alien to you, & mysterious.

LABOR POEM #2
Kibbutz Gesher Haziv, Bananas

I crouched down. The leaf and the dried leaf. Not
a machete, more of a chef's knife. Alone
in the row. The dried, the rotting, the leaf.
The sap. Thought I saw a tarantula,
me or someone else. Stains. Alone, after
a week, a book that I tried, or someone else
ahead in the next row. Not romantic after
a week. The sap stains, the slice at the base. Not
trees, a prehistoric grass. A book I tried
to think about. The rotting between the trees,
not trees. I crouched down. Chef's knife, stains, everything
brown. The next row, leaf, a tarantula
under, me or someone else, the next. A book
I tried, everything brown. Not after a week.

DAUGHTER SONGS

I am always thinking about time:
that fluid or pool where our minds swim. Like if I see trees, it was
the other tree I saw, or the wind hissing through them, and what
I want to say the wind says better. Take, for instance, a time
when the Stevie Wonder song from 1972 comes on, and dissolves on the
    tongue as if it was
a filo dough of his voices and supple Rhodes chords layered one at a time
from every point in your life you ever heard it—his surge of innocence,
I love I love I love I love every little thing about you, can you locate a time
where it stands still, by itself, not pouring backwards and forwards its stream
    of confidences?

And doesn't everything that sweet feel like long ago,
like echoes, caught in the honey trap of the past? As if it must
leave before it has arrived. But arrive you have, who still belong
to yourself, looking up surprised as I come or go,
straining away from my memories, towards you. Lifting you when you wake, I
    have
no container for that feeling, the new skin, the climbing onto me; the
    photograph
won't hold this. So we slough after you, in our frazzle to preserve your
small unblemished body from all the blunt things. Yes but the memories,
    they're
already mounding up around you, and who has a shovel, and finally all that's
in my hands is a song, chorusing back through the leaving and the left,
which I'm carrying, for any chance to sing you.

*Songs for my Daughter has as its endwords of each line the words from the Simon and
Garfunkel song "Bookends." This is a form I learned from Terrance Hayes.*

5

SKY MATH

How like a window
the mountain shakes you. Substitute
you for heat and the other handholds – granite, breath,

noise, fear – the bulbous
parts of the roots you climb. A rock-
shaped quietness empties the bowl, what's audible

from all that twitches
above tree-line. This empty page
of sky is made of you, of sound but exceeds it.

How could it be that
you find yourself looking down to
where the ones who came before you, who held their breath

and bathed you, got stuck
and stayed there? How could it be that
you can't just pull them up with you? Those trees scooped still,

bleached into bone, bleached
into one noun as big as all
of it, elsewhere without going. This anywhere

abiding here, this
half-inflated windsock, less than
orange, the sun-rescued hue of it, this orphan.

There are no bodies
on the chairs now but they, aloft,
the chairs, talk to each other when stirred, like you do,

pushing their complaint
through keyhole, behind which the snow,
the open mouth of snow. The nothing song of it

as if it could be
history, the grasses combed flat
under new antennae, their sharp green perfections.

It melts now, daily,
the monastery door. What cloud
made its bed here? What ladder? What poem climbing down.

COLLISION

1.
The night he left
the ice cream in the refrigerator by mistake
was the night I'd had enough.

God damn it all to hell.

The vanilla potage seeped out
of the carton, pooled on the shelf,
and clung to the ledge until
it spilled over. Drip, drip,
into the shelves of the door
between jars of sauce and pickles.
I swore he'd have to clean it all up.

Is love always an exaggeration?

2.
Chain link fence. Ball point pen.
Houndstooth coat. Every word
uttered is a violent collision:
vocal chords fracture the air,
the tongue pushes off the palate,
lips compress.

3.
Why is it never enough to say *I'm sorry?*

4.
On the corner of Franklin and Riverside,
a silver minivan strikes a middle-aged man.
He ascends with astounding speed,
yet he observes the glint of the yellow aspen,
surveys the Virginia creeper below.

Never one to worry, he reaches the vertex
with a kind of flair--two full revolutions.
He thinks of the last time he made love
to his wife, so incredibly satisfying
in all that wonderful, slippery rightness,
and then he descends.

THE AWAKENING

It doesn't matter what once was
because now what stands

she can't beat back. In the frozen
section of the grocery store she'll

hesitate when she catches her reflection.
The same pause while she pumps gas.

When she drives downtown between skyscrapers,
churches, courthouses, and arenas, she'll

realize just how confident concrete is.
And then back at home, she'll

hear the sense talking—a yielding, smiling,
ever so compliant face talking. On the piano

the children will bang out the sound of reason.
Even the pet parrot hung in its cage

will say, *Come back to sleep, come back
to sleep*. Some mornings she'll

stare into the bathroom mirror, naked, and wonder
if she can undo each brick, pick at the mortar

with her fingernails as if it were a scab. She'll
search the reflection for sledgehammers and axes,

imagine striking and toppling. And if she could
level the joints, the pillars, the beams,

reduce them all to splinters, she might
realize what once was, never was. And then she'll

make her way to the kitchen, to the eggs, to the juice glasses,
to the china plates, and then back to her bed.

FOLLOW-UP APPOINTMENT

You'd think that inside the open incision
the tumor would declare itself
as obvious, a hard pit
darkish and persistent,
unwilling to let the flesh go,
but the surgeon explains that cancer
looks like healthy tissue,
that's why the marker with its metal hook
gets pushed in,
why she must excise widely
to keep the margins clean.
Similar, I suppose, to skirting
around a volatile dog
or how, just this afternoon, I kept
a good distance between me and the guy
dancing outside the gas station,
who asked, "How're you doing, Sweetheart?"
and I said, "Fine, thanks,"
and felt, actually, a little happy
even as I glanced quickly away,
my body still visibly female,
all of me as yet intact,
even my blonde-dyed hair.

NATURE POEM

I don't understand what I'm looking at
That tree is full of swollen eyes

My hair feels terrific
Under the heat of my blow-dryer & God's love

If he ever falls in love & moves away
& everything turns out okay

It'll be good to see the butt of another cowboy

That mountain in the background keeps looking at me
The season is open

I could live in the lies he tells
I mean I could crawl up & die inside

The tree outside my window, leaning

Idling below Departures in a rental car
Let's stop for a while & never restart

I don't understand the women we're looking at
Are they flowered men

Stay with me a little longer
Whole chronologies are occurring to me

The brothers are sitting beside each other
I'm interested in becoming sick of them

There still isn't no one here

*

Flash forward all these years to Virginia

Weekends way down deep—New Orleans
Charleston, Savannah, Atlanta, mhmm

You could never be real to a place like this

& I'll never see him again
& we'll never be Facebook friends

Or I'll stop exercising & the news will end

Old Virginia singer stop singing
I've felt too much today

All the raw material in the world can't save me

I'm about to be thirty & over & I'm afraid but
Not about how I won't get any taller

SONG

It could never be evening here
You have your choice
Bright as day day or black as black night

I keep seeing the nature guide everywhere
He has He-Man muscles and Cinderella hair
I think he's real but I don't really care

No you can't borrow my sweater
Though I'm not using it
And you can't have a bite of the enormous burger I'm not going to finish

What I assume you can't assume
My melodic self is hiding underneath the couch cushions
Wilting like dinner in a pan

It's my America and you can't try it
What's the name of the place I'm staying
Everyone calls it something different

I don't know if it's a town or a alley or what
        The names of the grocery store chains
        Or the number of the interstate

The road along the water curls like someone else's hair
This ocean is a river
I can see the other side

Roll up your window
        This car is a box where my voice can grow
Probably someone will call soon to close a deal

When one of us swaggers through the office
Big and lucky and smug
It makes us worried God will come

And when He does
With his older-than-Old-World anger
Our smiles and tans will fade

He'll churn the snow-blessed mountains and break the hikers' legs
Or so we've heard it said

Or so we've been afraid

And our fear is the shape of everything in the world
Except what our eyes have seen
Oh I know

Let's get really drunk and put our love on the table
And pass around overheard overused moments like moist towelettes
And hurt each other's feelings in the morning in abbreviated halting utterances

I can hear the sun
      It's giving off its qualities
Coming out of its silence

It sounds like a car giving up
      Let's get inside it
            And drive it higher than we're supposed to go

THE PROMISE

The night we brought her home
the crickets stopped chirping.
Night filled the driveway. Silence
walked us to the door.

Bond, bondage, Band-Aid, binge.
I only remember
the green chair, my nipples
bleeding, waking to a fist
on my chest.

The sun didn't rise
for six months. The chair, the remote,
the trash fiction, pages bent from touch.
The fist now a grip,
a new scab forming.

Each week was a year
of Legos in the disposal
stuffed animals for dinner
lunch at midnight
with too much wine.

Bond: a tie, a connection
a knot wet with tension.
Bruises form from the inside.
If you knew the outcome
would you promise anyway?

You imagine alternate endings,
begin to write again:
living will, disability, inheritance,
you plan for death and retirement
in that order. Small print, signatures.

You've traded your words for some reward.
The grasping fingers, the breath
against your skin. Is it enough? A name
you haven't earned
shadows your own. If you break,
does the promise?

AGAINST RETROSPECT

1. The Garden
Leaf, flower, needlespray.
Never decide while eavesdropping.

Hands drift open, cupping
contained mystery, the belly
a swollen drupe.

What I dreamed for my daughter:
a petal, unfolding itself to sun.
Another's passion. My terms.
Then I met her.

Lamp-smasher, berry-masher, world
spinning-the-wrong-way fixer-upper.
Put your shoes on
[Twirl thrice; hop like a cottontail. Pull
the sandals into the spokes of a sun]
Scattered in a splay of catclaws.
Sobs. A voice bleating
lateforwork, lateforgymnastics, lateforschool
Is collision ever quiet?

2. Coyotes
That first boy in that first truck, skin
prickling like a new star. What I imagined
was mine, pulled like a curtain over
what I never, frightened
of nothing but myself.

Memory changes the event.
Like believing, without suspicion
I could invent a child, even though
I know, when coyotes yip in the night
something is about to die.

3. The Fruit
It comes easy to some, composing
for another's pleasure. For others, it is metal
bending, the pit at the center clinging
to each threaded strand of fruit.
Put your shoes on.

Her skin is sticky with peach.
It hurts my words she says. She bares her teeth, shows me
the pit, cupped in her hand, cracked across the center.
We are out of time for words. I grip her wrist.
Wash hands. I pull her to the sink. *And then,*
Shoes.   On.

SILK SCARVES

The first time you came to my house
you brought some long silk scarves—
I wondered, and asked what they were for,
and soon enough you enlightened me.

How could you recite me like a poem
when others read only the prose of me—
it's always been that way between us,
two strange beasts circling each other,
doubtful that others of our kind existed.

You wore one of those for the gig at the Hill
the night you opened for that lousy band,
and even the bad boys at the back of the house
shut their mouths when you started to sing,
your Fender slung from a silken sash,
black lace gauntlets on your tender hands.

Not even the silk worms in their trees in China
know what you can do with six feet of scarf,
wrapping me up like a present to myself
in the silk of your merciful and boundless love,
silk fine enough to draw through a small ring,
soft as your voice whispering to the moon,
but strong as a steel cable when pulled upon,
and my breath catches at the back of my throat,
when I picture how afterward we'd embrace,
arms wrapping each other tight, silk scarves
forming a basket of light that contains us
in some place without a face to time.

CASSANDRA

when it all comes crashing down, and it *will* come crashing down
I don't want to have to be the one to say I told you so
don't take my word, even Yeats knew the center could not hold
though in *his* Dublin you didn't need a single app
and that's precisely how I figure it will happen
never mind the terrorist under the bed, look at me instead
for I am Chaos and you cannot see my face for all my heads
but you will recognize my arms and my aims
out of the roiling turmoil of your dreams
I am the Luddite who has you in his gun sight
I am the scheme of a billion ghosts in the machine
I am the magnetic pulse weapon frying networks
      like a child annihilating ants
      the seven-forty-sevens on nine-eleven
      the gears of the Mayan calendar running out of years
I am the sniper in the bell tower of your fears
I am Diebold democracy enslaving your children
      stamping their brows with a barcode
      and a hundred grand in debt
I am the pentagonal top secret that a child somehow hacks
I am the algorithm in some safe at Goldman Sachs
I am the hanging chad on which destiny hangs
      the white powder envelope in the mailbox
      of cost containment and calculated risk
I am the meltdown no one ever expects
the permanent blackout waiting to pop
the shoddy interface breeding like flies
      the viruses morphing faster than cures
I am the failsafe mechanism that somehow tanks
      the foolproof system foolishly depending on a system-proof fool
I am the chemical spill, oil spill, nuclear coolant spill,
      the fracturing spillway of a dam upstream
      spilling its guts though no one wants to hear
I am the gas leak cratering quiet neighborhoods in a flash
the dominoes set up to cascade at a touch
the tipping point on the blind scale of justice
I am the vital infrastructure no one wants to pay for
      the rust at its core whose name is legion
I am the blowback of no more available Prozac
      when the grid becomes the collective id
I am the migrating hordes moving northward
      darkening the complexion of pale plains

harboring from heat, drought and exhaustion
        arriving like a bill that's finally come due
and I'm coming for you, who think you are the exception
you who think you'll somehow muddle through
for you are soft as crabmeat in your techno-shell
white, cold and rubbery, molded human surimi
crippled by these things that you depend upon
soon you will need a device to wipe your ass
        when you cut your morning loaf
or one to hold your pud up when you piss
I am the entropic law that rules this universe
        like a bully overturning your board game
        a Santa Claus of gloom and ruin
and you brought this all upon yourself
pretending you could have it all and have it now
and you will have it all and have it now
and soon

CATALOGUE

1. Some of our best inventories of the Roman gods
    come from Augustine, who mentioned them only to
    show how arbitrary the old religion was. Abeona, who
    watches over the child's first steps away from home;
    Adeona, who brings him back safely. Himeros, god of
    longing. After school, I would walk to the library to
    write them down, into the thousands, one for every
    rock and stream, every stage of gestation and kind of
    sex, until the children found me there, too.

    The Romans called on four gods to help them remove
    a particularly stubborn tree—The Pruner, The
    Breaker-Up, The Burner, and The Carrier-Away.

    * * *

2. Thirty minutes into Psycho, Janet Leigh lies naked
    and draped on the bathroom floor, a shower curtain in
    her hand. It is black and white. She is the color of the
    curtain. The blood is actually chocolate syrup, which
    is now made from corn. The swirling drain fades into
    a close-up of her eye. She must hold the pose, naked
    and dripping for forty-two seconds. We watch with
    our pause buttons, delighting in the twitch of a lid,
    the nostril's slight dilation.

    The blood funnels counter-clockwise because of the
    Coriolis effect. The Lowland Scots called this direc-
    tion *widdershins*, which means *against the direction of
    the sun*. It also sometimes means clockwise. It can
    mean itself and the opposite of itself, like *sanction,
    dust,* and *impregnable.*

    * * *

3. The walls are never the problem. It is always the roof
    that needs replacing. In the whorehouses of Pompeii,
    ashes have preserved frescoes of the various positions
    available to customers. There were three female pros-
    titutes to every ten men in Pompeii. They were called
    lupae, wolves.

    There are also the crouching mothers and the perfect
    hands of children. But the thatch roofs burned on
    impact.

    * * *

4. In the third act of *Vertigo*, Jimmy Stewart gets thrown
    off Kim Novak's scent. We are expected to believe
    this. Her hair is de-bleached and un-bunned. She
    wears a pair of thick, ridiculous eyebrows. In real
    life Hitchcock wanted to turn her into Grace Kelley,
    whom he'd lost to the prince of Monaco. He dyed her
    hair and taught her to walk like a princess, or a block
    of ice. He never used her again.

    In real life Novak had an affair with Sammy Davis Jr.,
    for which they both received death threats.

                    * * *

5. Scraps of Sappho lie waiting in perfume jars and
    caves: bits of stored energy, plant, animal. We are still
    finding them. A nearly complete poem was found
    wrapped around the snout of a small embalmed croc-
    odile.

    It might have said, *I am more than your brackets and
    asterisks, more than the surprise of pronouns.*

                    * * *

6. The gooseflesh around your nipples. There is the
    broken one and the breaker. Sometimes it is that
    facile.

    There is someone here who looks *just like you*—he's
    got your eyebrows just right, your pigeon-toed walk. I
    would use him in my next film, if he were available.

LIVELY
for Galway Kinnell

A Sierra chipmunk runs along the creekside
alders trembling through the late afternoon—

Twelve of us gathered in the augury of evening cool.
You wore the linen shirt—rose madder,

a fugitive color, purple-red, and the white
linen trousers of your Squaw Valley summer,

listening for the language with life in it:
"There's something lively about poems written here."

By chance, weasels wriggled their way into both
our works that day, mine devouring a magician's doves,

yours featured for his active whiskery nose.
There was more about the nose, the sneeze

signifying a simplified orgasm, the truth
of the body. You never liked cliché,

such as, 'canopy of sky', and as for cliffs, fine,
once 'sheer' had been deleted: "I'm glad that's gone."
                              *
I remember your pressed and rumpled fabric—
The web of our life's a mingled yarn,

good and ill together. Frank
about your love of Shakespeare,

 "He may be at times archaic,
but he is not old-fashioned," you taught

the way a fly fisherman shadow-casts,
long circles of line widening the air

above the river, two flies, a hopper
and a dropper; one floats in the foam, the other

drifting below so the trout, eager by now,
Have two opportunities to bite.

You liked women. Loved, lusted, liked
creatureness of all sorts, its functions and glories—

the basic mud Cleopatra came from.
The glittering skin of the asp that killed her.
                              *
And in July my first year at Squaw, a Wednesday,
I wore a lavender Laura Ashley dress,

four of us squooshing on the couch — I'd written
about my spouse, his illness, his staggers and falls

and how, not why, I loved him: There's no explaining
attachment. The title, from the Scottish play,

an augury of thickening light, the rook- haunted,
owl-screeched wood, years too terrible to write about.

But in that present, you took my poem
and looking straight in my eyes, read the ending back to me:

"Run your hand over my forehead, love...
You are my haven...." Those lines I'd barely gotten through.
                              *
He let me hear them, in the voice
that was largely unchanged two years ago

under the umbrella, in the ripple of the creek.
As for that earlier time, it was rose madder,

fragile, mutable as any mortal thing.
In that moment, the twinkling of an eye

I did not know I would be changed.
As I write from here, Scorpio's fishhook

on the horizon and to its left, the teapot shape
of Sagittarius, the summer Milky Way

trickling between them, "the wages of dying
is love." Where I live, a great blue heron

will stand in the dawn wetland, while a piping
marsh wren sings its heart out.

BOOK OF REVELATION

And I heard as it were a noise of thunder,
one of the four beasts saying, Come and see.
And I saw. And Behold a white horse.

It was summer in Sweetgrass County
and I found an iron rack with five hooks
from a farrier in Big Timber where once
the horseshoes hung while the anvil grew hot.
At home in my Shakespeare kingdom it holds
five keys, one for each hook:

> Time, a wallet at his back, keeping alms
> for oblivion.
>
> Marina of no shores.
>
> Mistress Quickly warning Falstaff, her honeyseed
> rogue, I'll tickle your catastrophe.
>
> Sir John, dying, his nose, sharp
> as a pen, and his feet, cold as any stone.

These four may vary, slipped off
according to my mood, for I am a moody girl,
and interchanged. Life hangs by Ifs.
The fifth key, on the far right, near the door
will not be removed. It's that voice
speaking so often in words of one syllable:

Hang there like fruit, my soul, till the tree die.

"Time, a wallet at his back..." Cf. Shakespeare's *Troilus and Cressida,* III, iii

"Marina of no shores" Cf. Shakespeare's *Pericles,* V, i

"Mistress Quickly...." Cf. Shakespeare's *Henry IV,* Part Two, II, i

"Sir John, dying..." Cf. Shakespeare's *The Life of King Henry V,* II, iii

"Hang there like fruit..." This line from *Cymbeline,* V, v, spoken by Posthumus embracing his wife, Imogen, is said, variously, to have been Tennyson's *or* Wordsworth's favorite speech in all Shakespeare.

GEOMETRY

the architect at Salisbury cathedral
carved space to a room for longing

alone in the echoing stillness
the high vault of roof invites:
    lift, expansion, a sense
    of possibility

massive carved door with its ratio—
three to five, pleasing to the very cell:
    safety, strength, I
    becomes small

low ceilings, long halls, the smell
of old dust: I questions assumptions

this is also the gift of redwoods
shaped by wind and angles of shade

spiral of branches
math of perfect ratios

ordered twirl of pine cone and nautilus shell
matching coil of cochlea, the gong of tiny bones

the supple spirit bone that resonates
to the still minutes of the night

the swooping lift of swallow
the pause before it dives

the rin, ceremony of its ringing
the way breaking silence creates silence

THE STORY OF I

We become he and she.

He leaves and you becomes uncertain:

sometimes he, occasionally she, certainly not I.

Time passes, she trips often on we.

You sits alone with you in an airless room.

I and she stand against the ropes in separate corners,

swish water past bloodied teeth, wait for the bell.

He sends postcards with Japanese stamps.

We chisels dates on a stone.

I reaches often to touch the soft fontanel

and it closes and hardens to bone.

You waits, impatient and pacing.

We considers a new favorite chair.

She and you sign letters of agreement

and you brings you to the dance.

I eventually decides who you is:

she, you, I and we.

BALTIMORE TO ST LOUIS BY AIR

Crossing the air's great page,
where the poem experiences meaning,
meaning O'Keefe's clouds   repeat
clouds   bricked up to the horizon
or Magritte's sky   postcard
peeled from a window
or Rothko's black
insistent light,
dropped into the dark outside,
where in fact it is night,
the super bowl's about half over
and half the country is cheering
while I'm up in the air
leaving friends, returning home
to my half of the former life
identity checked, the body
and other things that carry me
x rayed and passed through
illusions of security and procedure
I pass through the air's great page
where the poem experiences meaning
and does or doesn't *land* I think *land*

IN WHAT VOICE

On the no-measuring stick, the increments
are rivulets and thermals, whether the blackbird
clucks or not, where the updraft of swallows occurs.
How does its small world make sense of the big?
In what un-measures? How does it handle
the way aspen leaves are to words
as bird-songs are to bird-song mnemonics.
Do consonants close its odd transcription?
If all its birds are singing, in what voice,
awkward as a rusty lock?

DREAMS, SLANG, COMPOST

The time has come for all the poems about
dreams to come out of hiding because
let's face it we're all sleep-deprived and desperate tonight.
I'll go first. I dreamed a bobcat
and a housecat
and a fat-trunked tree. Bob
stalks House—just playing?—No,
Bob's trying to kill House, he's got him
in his jaws, biting the base of his spine,
and House is gray and long-haired and he looks
like somebody's pet – Stop, Bob, stop! and
Somebody throw a rock! Throw a rock!
No one is throwing a rock....

And while we're at it, let's trade slang
across the generations. We're all poets here,
doesn't that make a stronger tie than accidents
of birthday? I'll go first.
When I was a youth and we wanted to leave or quit,
we'd say "bag it" as in: "We've studied
for half an hour already, let's bag it and go smoke a J."
Do they still call a Marijuana cigarette a J?

This morning, there were three huge piles of compost
in the hotel parking lot, steaming in the bright sun
when I pull up the blind. I wanted
to go over there and smell their scent of slow-
burning earth. Have you ever put your hand on a compost pile?
So much heat at the surface, imagine how hot inside.
Gary Snyder says poetry is compost. It takes
all the detritus and dreams and undigested bits of our lives
(single and collective)
and transforms them into rich fertile soil
that can grow nourishment for us all, giving us
a way forward – what we need to survive.

Which is why I suppose that now there are poems
about the Internet and cell phones and Twitter –
the new slops and peelings of our age,
trying to become something that can feed us.

LYRIC, SQUAW VALLEY 1832

Can you picture it?

Those immortal aspens stand sentinel

on the southern lava flank

     overlooking the great marshy meadow where unrolls

the spring-flooded creek in lazy curves and out there

        the women bend and dig sweet onion, camas root,

fill their willow baskets with this abundance while

     laid on supple hides thrown over bristly Mahala mat

to keep them safe contained, the babies gaze

        wide-eyed at swallowtails hovering close to see

if these little ones are blossoms or perhaps potential mates before

     ascending to the hilltop where

they'll waltz together in the dazzle-light of noon.

O POEM

Ravish me! Be every unsayable word that's left
Or each and every word before it was
A word or when a word had only
Its sound for meaning, when they would string
Themselves into rhythms so interior
To the surface of things the soul
In everything was unavoidable
Though there was no single sound
In the mind for it but every sound together
The deep resonance—fan of the world, invisible
Wind coming and going in the trees, speaking,
Each thing a throb of color, a motion
Interwoven, articulate inarticulation,
Awakening the mind to itself—o Poem,
My ears are hungry, my heart is a backwater,
Make me dumb to anything that is not
Sound working the wordless fields
That mind can only bear witness to—
I want the pure ineffable, I want to hear it
When next you would ignore my foolishness.

FOR CHRIS

The night goes on forever,
But there are pockets in it,
Here and there. They come and go.
They're not always bursts of light.
Sometimes they're just holes in God,
Which is what makes everything
So difficult. Who can tell
The situation we find
For ourselves with that kind of
Topology at bottom?
Wasn't it better when it was
Great turtles all the way down,
And better when love and soul
Could room together and words
Could sing the huge darkness bright?
No, I don't like endless night;
I don't like the holes in God.
But all in all, you love me—
More than good enough for dust.

FAMILY

My cousin Lexi wants to play Scooby Doo, which means
she and Erika want to ride around on my back even though
they aren't ten and it isn't fucking cute anymore.
But you can't tell young girls that. That will come

soon enough and from their friends. If I speak in English
while they ride me, they jab me in the side. I can say
"Ruh roh." I can say "Scooby Dooby Doo." The grownups
are busy in the other room. If I won't play,

they tell my parents, who send them back to me
with orders. And don't get me wrong, I don't belong
with the adults either. They sit stiffly,
discuss taxes and how to handle the farmland.

My grandmother starts to cook a ham, the smell
rushing from the kitchen. Needless to say, I hate ham.
When dinner is done, grandma asks me to show her how
to check if her email is broken. Their computer is so slow

I can't tell. It might be loading. While we wait, my cousins
demand to play Scooby Doo. Again. Grandma asks
if I've gained weight. I tell them I've left my phone
in the car just to take a break.

When I get back, my grandpa wants me to weed
the lawn and cut down low branches above the shed.
And when I ask my Mom if I have time
before we head out (hint hint) he says he'll even pay me.

I know what he'll give me, a couple bucks –
good money back in the dust bowl.
I'd rather do it for free. I know I'm not
a good grandson. I know I've gained weight.

DECEMBER, PADRE ISLAND

We drove down the isle in the minivan
until we couldn't see anyone
and then we just kept driving.
I had to imagine the girls. A fourth beer

then a fifth – my brother, on his second, seemed calm,
serene even. My parents had, to their knowledge,
never seen me drunk. Nowhere here to hide
the bottles or the boredom. I just stared

out as we bumped down the beach.
When my dad asked what I was thinking,
I sighed with depth, said "nothing", and waited.
My father called this look my poetry face.

But truthfully, I was daydreaming
of easy, seasonal beauties, out
for Spring Break. I wanted to be as drunk
as them, drunk enough to take my shirt off

and wave it in the air. More staring.
Old grizzled fisherman, their still lines
in the shallows. My mother took photos.
I was so drunk. Where were my loose,

lost women? We reached the end
of the beach, filled with huge
Mexican families and their minivans.
I don't know why we all went that far.

ASPEN

I'd like to know how a life without mind
can shake almost always in every cell
and still seem good with itself.
Could be the foliage, each wafer
with a dark side and a light side,
rippling in the wind's lathered score,
green harmony anywhere you stand.
Maybe the rawboned branches,
chalice silver flecked with tarnish,
whose peeled staffs staked the hearts
of werewolves, whose acrid marrow salved
wounds of the Cree. Or the common underground,
solitary rakes bound by a root pact
too deep for fire. And what mind anyway
could render the voice of the other so unmeddled,
abide the frenzied and the bitter, the reaper,
with a mettle whose bark you would drink from,
whose leaves you would lay on your tongue.

THE CLONE

No one recalls whose idea it was;
we missed you in different ways.
Yet even at first rendering
the body was all yours
down to neckline and navel,
whistle and wink, beryl blue vein.
That copy didn't know me
but thought she might like to.

So they fused in shared facts and footage,
the girl with the catfish at summer camp,
a rainy bike ride down the coast of Maine.
Those who knew you a bit
from the office, the book club,
were pretty sure, but the weave
was still too loose for specialists
and her impersonations
different enough from yours.

So they added the power on her own
to gather and twine every thread
by touch and talk, fashion and salvage,
even what no one ever knew.
But she knew
it was yours not hers
and that showed through.

So they went to where the singular mind
clings to itself, grieves early its own loss,
flings itself on a heart that isn't flesh,
invents a soul.
Finding there what was ever only yours
they blew it into her
and you rattled in her bed,
missing some memories
as after a grim sleep or long war,
but feeling yourself,
with fear and free will.

So I asked them to make two more
of me: one as you always wanted—
festive, impetuous, orchids wild but tended;
one as I wanted for you—
less knowing, more curious to be known.
And now you can choose
among the three of us.

MOTHER'S FOLKLORE

Purple root bent
into the crook of a tree;
granite boulders unraveling.
A rhyme anyone's mother
would hum as a translation
for the wounds we never
knew we had.

We call them "ten sharp faces
folded with age," call them
slices of reticent light
hissing with numbness
and some look *into* each other
as if sitting for coffee
with the one who knows you best.
I was barely there
and still, their eyes gave off
an immaculate howl, if they had
mouths, which some do, and
most all of them do.

I couldn't understand then,
who were those men
we called Duendes
and why my mother smiles
when I ask her in the ivory
stillness of that room about their
green boots trudging our nights
away in burlap sacks,
splashing their liquid faces
into the damp earth.

DESERT: AN IMAGE

Folding our faces into
thin strips called derivations
of emotion as we cross the Nogales,
the senseless tearing begins
in day that groans like those ancient
rusted engines kicking over.

These are the innards of hallucination,
how the world is only halves to us:
as in plums pregnant with violet meat,
or the self-mutilating ritual
of casual laughter among friends.

Walking aimless through the desert
after a few days, our mouths
swollen with joy, or light,
those plum trees dancing
half of themselves away.
How dumb we were,
endlessly searching.

(Saturday draft)
AT THE SNOW LINE IN SUMMER

There appeared again
a little thinking cloud—; it was trying
        to figure out how to hover. Just to the right
of the peaks, some ancient flapping
            over the world eggs of the granite,
    fire striations after the glacier.
Just to the right of the mind, pines pushed up
from below...*scrrrrrip!* A million years pass.
        Nets of *letharia* drop
from the ponderosa. The gods hold back,
    deprived of terror.
        —*What is it now, Mrs.?*
        — *Not sure what you mean by now.*
        —*You were caught again in the nameless*
            hour till all of life seemed wrapped in it

That eagle wears its shadow eagle
    on the ground, coasts in the thermals,
barely flaps over the petro-fabric...
Bolds, givens. Toxic hours & mute money—
    & lately you hath
        gotten bossy at thy demanding job.
    In summer snow, pinched

nevering bulbs pushing up like Moscow
churches. Some spikes
        of cold might heal your hurry.
    Effort of vision reversal— but here you are,
still upright at the edge of sound...

AMY HOFFMANN

ODE TO THE LETTER O

You come from the eye as
an Egyptian hieroglyph
but you are of the mouth
making your shape
to utter your sound
an onomatope
self-contained and whole
a hole
a vowel
a word
a complete thought.

How many O's
have come out of mouths
in this hour or day or ever?
Do you loll in the air
hooping yourselves over
self-important I's
in an invisible letter orgy?

You land on the page
by someone's hand
so unround or overlapping
or curling into yourself
as if to proclaim that Plato was right
perfection cannot exist
in script, or even Courier
or in the lead from the foundry

yet you buoy up J and Y
a yellow helium balloon
and you are twin oxeyes in bloom
one orbit
and the empty pails inside
the two ends of
sorrow

at the end of you
the lips become a kiss
O! Magnificent O!

I want to slip you on my hips

and around my tongue
and feel each O ever said
into my body's hum
and echo them
back into the O steeped air: O!
Over and over again.

AMY HOFFMANN

AUBADE

a space
between
exhale
and inhale
expanding
expanding
vacant, no, lush,
lined with felt
coil of copper
contained
in sleep hush
of umbra
cochlea maps
an empty spiral
filled up with
nothing

the egg
of you tucked
against my sepalled self
the skein of half sleep
ravels around us

here the now is everything

but I can't push
against the buried
sun for long
or keep you wound
around the
stem of night

then the fracturing

you will uncoil
& bound
from me to unfasten
the sugar
bowl sky

INTERVIEW WITH SHARON OLDS
BY NICOLE SEALEY

Awarded the San Francisco Poetry Award, the Lamont Poetry Prize, and the National Book Critics Circle Award and shortlisted (twice) for the T.S. Eliot Prize, Sharon Olds is a poet among poets.

In July 2011, I had the honor and pleasure of studying with Olds at Squaw Valley. I've been an Olds fan since *Satan Says*, but must admit I was a bit intimidated about meeting the woman behind the words. I found that she is not only "a poet of sex and psyche," but also a teacher of great warmth and generosity.

Late last year, Sharon Olds and I extended a conversation started that summer on matters of community, craft, and creativity.

Nicole Sealey: There's something to be said for belonging to a "community" of writers.

Sharon Olds: When I squawk in the valley, it is deep and sweet (and scary) to know that someone—eleven or twelve someones—will listen to the work, really listen each morning... It is far from lonely.

I recently saw a snapshot of Lucille and me by the lake at Squawk!-Washoe Valley Community of Writers. You can't tell, but I'm taking an insect off of Lucille's sweater. When a spider or ant or any bug crawled on her, she would call "Sharon! Sharon!," and I would cleave unto her side. Imagine! To be a knight-errant of Miss Lucille Clifton!

NS: Squawk!-Washoe Valley Community of Writers?

SO: What did the people native to the valley call the valley? Our guide David Lukas told us the Washoe lived above the valley and came down into it to hunt and fish. So, I have started thinking of it as Washoe Valley. And since our late-comer tribe of writers—the Halls and all of us Hallettes, singing back-up—blurts out a song a day for a summer week, here, I've thought of it also as Squawk! Valley... thus the Squawk!-Washoe Valley Community of Writers!

NS: What makes for a good "song," what are your craft dos and don'ts?

SO: Craft rules for myself are: take vitamins, dance, walk, obey your California Chardonnay limits, work at taking good care of myself, especially the spirit. I think my craft principles are pleasure and accuracy and play.

My dangers (don'ts) include: sentimentality, self-pity, cliché, self-parody, and getting in the way of where the first draft wants to go. The first draft should go where it likes, it should have its civil liberties.

NS: What do you think of rule number two of Lawrence Jay Dessner's *How to Write a Poem*: "Never treat your reader without respect"? The *what not to dos* include: do not lie; do not force your reader to guess what's going on; do not speak to your reader as if you were Moses; do not tell your reader how to behave; and, do not show off.

SO: I love the idea of treating with respect anyone who might chance upon a poem of mine! Though the "Never" makes me want to find a way for the poem to treat a reader without respect in a way delicious to us both! And here's something funny—after the "Never" and the "do not"— "do not" is "do not speak to your reader as if you were Moses!" Sometimes—not in my poems so much, but in many poems—the point is that nothing is going on, or nothing clearly tellable is going on, or that a poem is trying to embody something mysterious! It isn't necessarily that there's "a plain story" which is in danger of being obscured.

      I'm not sure if I agree with the basic tenor of "force your reader" (with free will, anyone can toss the magazine across the room after line one). And, I do like showing off, so though I think I'm in sympathy with the underlying intent of these rules, I don't think I can be in that club.

"My dangers (don'ts) include: sentimentality, self-pity, cliché, self-parody, and getting in the way of where the first draft wants to go. The first draft should go where it likes, it should have its civil liberties."

NS: One of my favorite poems of yours is "I Go Back to May 1937." What's your favorite Sharon Olds poem?

SO: I have little riffs I like in different poems. A half line here and one-and-a-half lines there—a phrase, one which sounds to me like a "real poem," when the music is equal to everything else… I call these my Seamus Heaney *Jr.* (very Jr.) moments. It would be of interest to me to see whether these lines and phrases are passages of simile. I wouldn't like my poems much were it not for simile—the unconscious part of what I do. I am a happy camper when one of those passages passes through me onto the page.

      There are also poems I am so glad I wrote—and you know how it is, how little control we have over what we write. I think I have thought, wrongly, that other writers, "real poets," have more control over or are more conscious of what they write in first draft. But maybe all of us are just sitting there, hoping to stay out of it enough that the pen will be the spoon stirring the soup in the appropriate circles.

NS: At what point in your process is truth abandoned for the imagination? Is it ever abandoned?

SO: I've come to understand that I'm an autobiographical, narrative, formal poet—as well as a poet writing about joy and pain and the human in general, and a writer of odes and poems about war. I don't have any imagination. I have *image*-ination. But, I don't really have it—it has me, or is me, my brain is wired in the service of the simile, which may be where the mysteriousness, a certain kind of non-strict connectivity comes into my poems.

NS: Are you sometimes hesitant about revealing *too much* or are you at a point where *too much* isn't even a concern?

SO: If what I'm writing about is my business (or, I feel as though it's my business), then I'm not sure what "too much" would be. I love the word "reveal," but I've become increasingly aware that what we do is *invent*. In my case, invent as close a copy or record—an account, witnessing—of some actual personal thing/dream/news event as I can. And to try to get the *feel* of it. The poem seems to come from the back of my mind, down my arm, and through the pen in light of my mind and heart and flesh.

Reveal *too* much? If it's my story, and not someone else's who wouldn't want it told (this doesn't seem to apply to presidents, generals, or parents), then the only danger might be to reveal more than the art can bear, ferry, carry, cherish, an imbalance between the freight and the carrier—big strong heavy freight, frail carrier.

THE LEMON PICKERS OF AUBURN

we count on others, not always
        this is the ebb & break of fortune
with a quiet unloading of the groceries

his face, a child's jawline
        a stroke of yellow roadside
freshly shaven all around, I see the tree

as he grabbed my purse watering the lawn
        & weeping with lemons
the register of wire inches away

from my hands to see a laughing jewel
        a hummingbird hovers, eyes
dart from forehead to chin to noseline

looking to drink, I chase him
        to his car, yell through silver glass
& reach out to take it, am I to blame?

THE CRONE SPEAKS OF CALIFORNIA
In support for H.R.1116 & S. 598

Softness pours out on her kitchen table
      in unlit candles, and empty plastic cans.
The crone makes soup over the stove
      and drops half of a chicken in the pot.
We watch her walk around the house
      as if her boots were tied to the kitchen
by a single thread, silvering behind.
      To her, the child died in a lover's arms.
Does one define this type of *hunger?*
      Could Hadrian have asked The Silent
this instead of *man* and *woman*? We know
      too much of human sin and submission,
but to understand a grieving woman
      and her guilt requires a new compassion.

APPLES, SWIMMERS

There's a blindness in my memory.
       An apple growing over the neighbor's fence.

There is a man singing in the alleyway mostly deaf, but knows the songs,
       knows how the timbre should feel in his throat.

There is a swimmer addicted to distance, waiting for the body to fail.
There is a man sawing to roots of the past so he may attempt to see with
   clarity.

My wife tells me to join my brother for dinner. To sacrifice an evening with
   love
for an evening with a different kind of love. I do not want to be obligated.

There is a train leaving the valley.
       Above its exhaust plume there is a capturing of alpenglow.

There is a sculpture, the artist now dead, forgotten in a friend's attic.
       It holds a type of perfectness that cannot be acknowledged.

My brother is late. He is in love again. It makes me smile, for now my role
is more equitable than dependent. He does not let me into his apartment
   but
says it is small, messy, perfect.

I want to open myself to him again. We are navigators of avoidance.
Ubiquitous cherpas. It will take a few beers.

There is a horse on the last wild mountain.
There is a sound of falling water that never hits bottom.

My wife does not call me. I want to call her but don't. She says
this is the cheapest therapy we can afford. I imagine our two sons
playing in a fountain as evening settles in. Shirts off.
The quiet streets fill with their laughter.

I know my brother is my equal. Endured the same crucible.

There is a man listening to the singer in the alleyway.
       Listening to an extinct type of humility.

There is an elder cardiologist with a pacemaker,
       the model so old he cannot enter certain rooms to perform surgery.

OF BEGGARS AND KINGS

I am thinking of an artist I cannot remember.
Reminded of language's levity, how we appropriate more than inherit.

I am thinking as I arrive from the shower leaving so much behind.
The shadows of cascade. Of equivocal engineering.

There are reasons I do not like to come to conclusion.
It is not the sea we take with us, but a bit of its sand maybe a tan.

I am thinking of how there is no good way to approach beauty
other than to corrode it with touch or let it desert your thought.

I am thinking of the crocodile's deliberate case of my grandparents'
Floridian lake. How the sun sets differently for us all.

I do not want to say goodbye. They will depart.
My wife and kids may never meet them. Only introductions through photo.

I am thinking not out of loneliness or of regret, but as one who knows
only a fraction. New to the devices of birth and denial. My sons

in their superhero costumes and endless enthusiasm battle over victories
and calamity they sense at distance. Sense as a matter of human condition

that spins but does not break into altruistic countenance.
Nor does the vitality lecher off the chasm of asperity.

There is a statue I have never seen. I am told of its softened beauty.
How it was broken into impermanence.

How the blind neighbor rubbed his hands upon it as if a religious relic.
How his hands are calloused by its transpiration. As if a father, or

cloud humming through summer. There is a child picking blackberries
with a basket, with a mind, with a river racing to the foot.

I'm thinking about how we all speak to emptiness differently.
Some gently, well practiced. Others in fits of anger.

I'm thinking of the artist whom so vacantly slipped my lips.
Only the warmth of proximity. Now as cool as stone.

ROLLED-UP TRIPS

Two five-pound barbell plates and
a bar of soap from The Muse Hotel in Times Square.
These were the last things I ever gave my father.
They tucked easily in the casket.

I transported Frank from Vegas to Hillside Memorial,
the only place I could afford, high in the marble wall
close to where his parents stayed.

Dad has new neighbors since I last saw him.

A woman in her mid-fifties to his right,
and another woman below
whose plaque reads,
She loved her bling and she wore it well.
To his left, *I'd rather be playing my drums,*
and over the rail, *Aces and Eights.*
The casino never closes in Acacia Gardens.

Vegas has come back to him.

The bar of soap so he could smell nice for the ladies,
and the weights he loved to lift.
Mostly, I wanted to add ten pounds back to all he had lost.

Rolled-up trips: three of a kind dealt in the first three cards.

PAX

Our cat's eyes virescent and yellow
dilate around the time she starts to seizure.
Then she attacks her own tail with
a violent whipping and hiss
that turns her into a cyclone,
an Ouroboros from hell.

Pax has a feral background, that is to say,
her grandfather is also her father.
Not a problem for cats.
She was bottle fed by a couple felons,
students of mine at the rehab who
found her by the side of the freeway.

She spits out the expensive medicine we had
compounded for her at the pharmacy in Encino.
I'm going to hire an exorcist
or get her cognitive behavioral therapy
so that each time she intends harm to herself
Pax attacks the bully orange cat next door instead.

No one wants to say the word schizophrenic.
She hallucinates her warrior self but spends
all day in the garden eating white butterflies.
She once went one on one with an earthworm.
Let's just admit it.
This shit is normal for cats.

Besides, aren't we all a little self-terrorizing,
biting our nails and grinding our teeth?
I scratch my skin till it bleeds,
hide my hands under long sleeves.
Pax has a lot to teach me.
Don't make a rival of your extremity.

ILLUMINATIONS

Tree-like rises up the T,
though it is not green. It shades
a cherub on the left, symbol of pure
erotic love. An uncertain beast,
medieval concept of rhino or hippo,
tank-like and tusky, charges away
on the right, symbol of strength,
earthly might heavy as artillery,
a cannon dropped single-bodied
from its cast. Pages later, fruit,
grain, and vegetables spill
from the cornucopia of a G.
At this point in the story, their god
has blessed the people with
procreative love, a wealth of children
born after war chased war's
fortifications, swords, and arrows
from this now-peaceful land.
The only borders they know are those
of fertile ground, edges of rich soil
where they have harvested what fills
the capital-letter-turned-horn-
a-plenty. All this conveyed in ink,
the illuminated manuscript's giant
ciphers, allegories interpreted where
they hang on letters in a language
I do not know. There is much more
in this tome to figure out—
from a letter not common between
the book's and my alphabets
that golden bird rising, rising.

AFTER BEING ASKED, WHILE CLEANING UP FROM A DINNER PARTY, WHY I DO NOT KEEP A COMPOST PILE

Decay. The one-word answer as I slop
the wet towel over the countertop, its slate,
granite, that will be here even when I'm not.
The cabinet's full of appliances that might
outlast me—their plastic shells at least,
even if motors break down and the blender
or ice cream maker no longer swirls
new foods into being. But that banana,
not here from the store a week, turns black.
The red pepper's seedy core needs only
a few August days to look like some infected
organ plucked from my body and dropped
on an O.R. floor. Less for this avocado half.
Against decay, though, I wouldn't choose
to be the broken blender, no electromagnet
spinning its servos and gears, mere shell still here.
The countertop: let me be the countertop,
lasting. Or let its granite accept a chisel
carving out my name and a pair of dates.

AT SAINT JOSEPH'S ORPHANAGE

little girl like quaking grass
forlorn in a dorm
filled with beds

the nuns say *God doesn't*
want to see you naked
wear panties for weekly bath

little girl rolling down hill
mommy ran away and daddy
couldn't catch her

Christmas stocking filled with
walnuts, orange and a prayer
Hail Mary, hail mother

nuns can't be mommy
her story written in the clouds
and what about the bees?

eight million flower visits
to make a pound of honey

CORVUS CORAX

Her interview was a bad first date. He wore salon hair, Italian loafers, and gold chains; looked more like a car salesman than a city manager. But she wanted to leave Modesto where the Water Wealth Contentment Health arch was next to the Taco Bell that won best restaurant in a chamber of commerce contest. When he called, she accepted and moved to Davis where the inbox was piled higher than her head. He told her, "I'm in negotiations with the POA and no way am I backing down with those cops. You're going to hear I'm a hard ass, a real SOB." Then he told her he had trained a raven to eat berries and oatmeal on his deck at home. She wondered how he had managed to get a raven to perch on his hand, return when called. Well, she thought, the common raven is as intelligent as a chimpanzee, so perhaps the bird trained him. When one Wednesday the raven didn't show and didn't return on Thursday or Friday, he told her he had looked everywhere, even put up posters, but no bird. She didn't know what to say. She knew there had been a neighborhood nuisance complaint and two police officers had responded.

dear karen in italy, dear alison in texas, dear marty and tom and ruth in new york

Sentimentality doesn't bother me.
– Major Jackson, "Mediating the Inexplicable"

this morning i was thinking of st. louis, how we couldn't wait to leave that place that seemed to us provincial, lost. how we abandoned, disbanded, as soon as we had the chance, sure that our real lives were about to begin.

i was thinking of how, for me, it became mythic so quickly, the place not where i was happiest — who is happy at sixteen? — but where i lived the life that seemed to me most true. yes, i was living in my mother's house in a room with two twin beds and three lime green walls and large daisies with blue centers cut from felt when i was twelve. but i was also living with all of you and with the belief that we were brilliant and beautiful and nothing but good was waiting for us out in that world just beyond our reach.

i was thinking of you, marty, who i loved before i knew how to love anyone, and the poem you wrote about the corners of the mouth. and you, alison, who i loved before i understood the ways that was even possible. thinking of us as genet's sisters, solange and claire in *the maids*, and how utterly you kissed me when the script required it.

i was thinking of that last year we gathered in our abandoned shoe factory, mythic in its own right, no place they'd let children go for art classes today. splintery wood floors, obsolete machines in the corners of empty rooms, odd ropes and pulleys hanging from the ceiling. steep iron stairs to the space where we learned beckett and pinter, played theatre games, the winter sun spilling through big casement windows as we stretched in slow mirrored motion. i was thinking of the enclosed garden we could get to only by climbing through another window, where an apple tree dropped its fruit to ferment in the grass.

i was thinking of david, dead from throat cancer; kay and candy, heart disease; our teachers and mentors, russell and charlotte and patsy and now brian, and how of course we thought that all of us would be here forever.

it's july, and the streets in the central west end look just as they did, or almost so. wide sidewalks shaded by the same sycamores and maples; large brick houses surrounded by the same large green lawns. streetlights that changed the shape and length of our shadows as we wandered the summer nights.

and i'm thinking of my daughter, the same age now as we were then, growing up in california. she killed a snake one afternoon, caught in some garden netting, and wrote a poem — *a snake and a half*, she said, *the crumpled, limp body / of a second snake, almost fully formed*, inside the body of the first. and i'm thinking of all of it — *the velvet blood and peachy glisten of just living / the broken bird neck of almost living* — and how there's nothing we can do anymore, nothing we could ever do, to change any of it.

WILLOW/WINDOW
after Anna Akhmatova; a variation with OULIPO

I was raised in checkered silk
in the cool nutlet of the young century.
I didn't care about human voices,
had ears only for the wind and the wing's call.
I liked burials and netherworlds, winter,
nestlings and nets of star.
But most of all I loved the willow.
My compass through long years,
the willow wrapped me in its cool brilliance,
sheltered me within its green light breath,
feathered my insecurity with drifts, drafts, rafts of dream.

The willow died first, something I couldn't imagine.
I am here, while only its stump remains.
Everything else returned to ash.
Now other willows call, up and down the riverbank,
willows that are strange to me.
Now other windows open onto the green night,
the dark sky swirled with unfamiliar clouds.
And I can only stand here weeping — as though a brood of us had died.

HALF LIFE 3, CLOSE-UPS

—my heart closed   each time I felt & when it opened   we were science
—Brenda Hillman

Please stop the car, the weather is doing everything.
Over there fearful black cloudbanks rise, on this side
clouds mountain-climb through bright orange to ash
and white pillars of light come down like stairs to some
thing—look back at the black clouds, count
one no two rainbow and the alpenglow glows
another orange across the green green valley.
Please stop the car, the animals are here, three
bison calves play tag while the old bulls
wallow off winter coats in dust, stand dark silk,
stop, stay with this, stay. My dad—you couldn't
not thrill him with anything outdoors—brought us
here to Yellowstone in 1946, we stopped and
watched a bear with her three cubs for hours.

Stay with the river at Clark Fork, brown this spring
as Big Muddy, edging up (I used a tree across it
to gauge) but still in its own unplumbed course—
you know they are turning the Mississippi? Do
you know how they turned the Colorado? We
went there in 1947, the gray embrace of the dam
made my whole body cold, then we went down
into Zion as Daddy named parts and shapes
of the earth all day, the inland sea drained away,
the Grand Staircase, the red sandstone carved by the
free flowing Virgin River, blind arches, alcoves,
hanging valleys, he named them all day.

Toward the end of his life the outdoors became
a slow and stopping walk with his cane to his office,
three city blocks on two Percodan. He listed his ailments
in two precise pages e.g.ruptured lumbar disc 4
chronic pulmonary obstructive disease chronic
inflammatory disorder metastatic prostate cancer etc.
the names, the shapes and parts, of the earth.

HALF LIFE 8, WITNESSES

I was here first/ before you were here, before/ you ever planted a garden
—Louise Gluck

the octopus with its divided, lobed, folded brain, tool use, problem
solving, how it just pulls off our electrodes
the reindeer in the Arctic night finding lichen and pee (enemy? mate?)
with its ultraviolet vision
the horse Yahweh told Job about
the dog York, who knew 46 hand signals and would go into any water
above freezing
the many-little-flowered yarrow which gives its oil to its neighbors
and the soil
the Clark's nutcracker, burying its annual 98,000 pine nuts so the ones
it doesn't eat can grow
the yellow legged frogs which don't get born because the nutcracker
feeds the tadpoles to its young
the largest bull elephants, the ones who cover the breeders,
killed for ivory
the cats Maggie and Emma, who teach games and rituals and a water
meditation
the cattle Temple helped; Jane's chimpanzees along their narrowing corridors
the California corn lily, toxic in all its parts, able to clone clones
that live hundreds of years
the sad neighborhood white tail deer
the San Francisco garter snakes hiding in marsh edges
the mother Iberian lynx who needs three rabbits a day

>Insert anywhere above some witnesses of your own

LAY IN THE SOIL

if the bird is singing, you know she risks her life
tanager's calling, listen before she flies
cold river overflowing
we don't have much time

granite going to crumble, it won't take too long
tanager's calling, listen her frightened song
cold river overflowing
by evening she'll be gone

river's overflowing, waters cold as skin
lay in the soil beside me, let the flood begin
afraid i'll drown without you
can't let that happen again

morning begs for sunlight, to fill the mountain sky
tanager's calling, listen before its light
cold river overflowing
dawn's chorus will set it right

lay in the soil beside me, this is where i'm from
tanager's calling, listen her frightened song
cold water holds my life now
long as the river runs

SINNER'S REMORSE

cairns on view in ruins
cairns in sierra snow
mourn a name, mourn our nicene savior
seven sins we own

cairns on view in ruins
son a common man
answer a name, mourn a savior
now we own seven

cairns on view in ruins
cairns in sierra sun
a man a son, our nicene savior
saves in our reunion

WILLOW
...dearest to me was the silver willow.
— Anna Akhmatova

(I) count every tree down and up the red gum street,
the eucalyptus butchered until forgetting its treeness
withers and dies, the planted replacement a weeping
willow, light green in July, long branching whiplike
wands, two neighborhood boys skateboard by, dare
the coach hounds three doors down, play lion tamer,
teasing, taunt them, tangle as the least of us prepare
for playground glory, blackberry bramble, bullyboy
bravado of checkered flags and fists, falls and skin-
kneed silence, compassion is a badge for losers, see,
poison oak-plagued cushioned landings, those black
eye bruisers, kin to the stump, where a winding stair
arises, built by Tim and Tom, three stories high, seven
years' labor, father, son, time and the willow flowing
        going   going   gone to light.

CALLIOPE

Home at noon, tiny iridescence, a shimmering, half-turned
body, long spike of a beak- I nearly missed him, this bird
on our path, hummingbird, resting- can it be? Almost always

unseen, they're a flicker or flashes of color, heart-beating
breast, undulating in midair, hovering above us, beat of wings
aligned with breath, muscle flexes under feather and bone,

invisible harmonies of design, nature, but the bird is unsteady,
wounded and precarious on the path to the river house. I go
indoors, put down my notebook, and return, still he's there, body

two inches long, pristine and infinite, territory of color upon color,
a royal robe, world map in miniature, olive flecked, sheen and gloss,
of green, the brown wings with charcoal grey, edged in reddish brown.

Sensing me, and startled, head and body twist away, his breast, white,
dark and olive, wine-red the center tufts, flanks awash in red and pink,
Why now, here, Truckee River and time, blue sky afternoon rushing by?

At dinner, David listens, thinks the bird is a juvenile. *Stellula calliope.*
'He may be injured, skirmishing with other males, their beaks long
and sharp, they clash, dancing those *pendulum-like, U-shaped dives.*'

Always in flight, after nectar, the birds named for Calliope, lyric muse
and mother of Orpheus, he who with his lyre charmed rocks and wild
oaks on the Thracian shore—how will this earth-stranded one survive?

Someone told me *there's no such thing as coincidence*, now at my door,
not the muse, but messenger of one who called me poet, who in dream
took my arm, guided me through rooms filled with histories and books.

In the dying light, his chest labors, heaves, as his energy ebbs and flows—
what may be done for him? Can he survive the cooling night? Accept
whatever happens, now go inside, let night and work honor the muse.

Jack Martin

AN INTERVIEW WITH CATHY PARK HONG
BY ERICA ZORA WRIGHTSON

Cathy Park Hong's work is fueled by her athletic imagination, leading us to places and times that are both absurd and terrifyingly familiar. She is the author of three books—*Translating Mo'um* (2002); *Dance Dance Revolution* (2007), which was chosen for the Barnard Women Poets Prize; and *Engine Empire* (2012). Cathy is a full-time professor at Sarah Lawrence College and teaches regularly at the Queens MFA program in Charlotte, North Carolina.

Cathy joined the poetry workshop staff at Squaw Valley Community of Writers for the first time in 2011, alongside Robert Hass, Brenda Hillman, Major Jackson, and Sharon Olds. I was lucky enough to attend her workshop in the beautiful valley that summer and asked her a few questions the following winter about her approach to poetry and the role of place in her work.

Erica Zora Wrightson: At Squaw Valley last summer, you spoke a lot about place. You described your muse as place or lack of and said that a sense of negation propels your work. Do you feel that your history and your personal geographies limit or enrich your work?

Cathy Park Hong: Oh, definitely enrich. It's who I am, why I write. First off, I think all poets feel this psychic lack, whatever that lack may be; poets need yearning to write. For me, an unsettled sense of place and language has shaped me as a poet. My personal geographies allow my imagination to travel and give me freedom to muck up language. The writer as outsider is such a boring cliché but it holds true for me. You learn to listen, gain empathy, and not trust restricted doctrines of language and law.

EZW: How early do you decide on setting when developing an idea for a new poem?

CPH: Early on. I like to imagine a setting first. I try to imagine where I would want my poetic voices to come from. It can be inspired by a photo I saw in a gallery or a scene from Ursula Le Guin's novel. For instance, in my upcoming third book, *Engine Empire*, I have a section that's set in a fantastical industrial boomtown that's reminiscent of Shenzhen. When I first began thinking of the setting, I imagined there would be a river that runs through it and unfinished high rises. Then I start filling it in with hawkers or a factory throwing out defect player pianos into the polluted river, or lovers walking through an aquarium of angler fish. I have to have some kind of mental architectural space and then I people the space with poems.

Because of my approach, my poetry as of late has been more narrative-driven. When I'm beginning a series of poems, I always feel like I'm blindly feeling my way into my unconscious, with only a glimmering flashlight of an idea. But then the world becomes more visible as I write. Right now, I'm returning to L.A., my hometown. I have no idea really what I'm going to write about. But I have several visual clues to usher me into it, as well—references like Hernandez Brothers graphic novels, Kara Walker's murals, and Mike Davis.

EZW: How important is your own biography in your work?

CPH: It's absolutely unimportant and totally important. I'm not interested in recording my own lived experience and prefer writing about imagined lives, although shards of my biographical life are certainly in the mix. But how I grew up, what I was denied, my privileges, my education, my observations, what I read and teach, completely feed my writing.

EZW: You won a *Village Voice* Fellowship for Minority Reporters and have written for *Village Voice*, the *Guardian, Salon, Christian Science Monitor*, and *New York Times Magazine*. Is it challenging to switch from journalistic writing to poetry and vice versa? How do poetry and nonfiction differ in their approaches and responsibility to the truth?

CPH: I don't write nonfiction so much anymore and I dearly wish I could return to it. But when I stopped writing articles, it was right around the time when newspapers laid off tons of writers. *Village Voice* is a husk of what it was and it's been like that for a long time. I loved journalism: it was challenging, exhilarating, and frustrating. And it was hard to leap between poetry and journalism but it definitely fed my poetry, maybe even more than teaching. I collected hard data, stories from strangers, jokes, random bits of dialogue.

> *"As far as truth telling goes, I think poetry and nonfiction are on opposite ends of the spectrum. I always tell my students to lie. Factual truths are inessential. But you must seek emotional truth through form, music, imagery."*

Because I was forced to harass strangers, beg them for stories, listen, read, be ahead of the headlines, I firmly believe that poetry should be connected to the world and that it should—in subject, form, tone, or mood—be timely. And I don't know if this is my original temperament or journalism developed this sensibility, but when I write poems, I'm more interested in the lives of others rather than plumbing my own selfhood.

As far as truth telling goes, I think poetry and nonfiction are on opposite ends of the spectrum. I always tell my students to lie. Factual truths are inessential. But you must seek emotional truth through form, music, imagery. If you become too wedded to facts, it stymies your imagination. It prevents your poems from stumbling into surprising moments. There are no happy collisions between a sewing machine and an umbrella on the dissecting table, as the old Surrealist saying goes. In nonfiction, of course, it's completely different. Now, I'm speaking purely from the perspective of reporting and not literary nonfiction, but it's an ethical responsibility to have every fact correct and accounted for, especially during this day and age of Fox and you know the rest. I started out as a fact-checker after all, which now appears to be an obsolete job position.

EZW: In your craft talk at Squaw Valley, you said that we are all migrants living in hybrid worlds. Do you see this as a function of technology, as something we choose or imagine, or is it inevitable?

CPH: All of the above. I think we've always lived in hybrid worlds, but now it's becoming more accelerated and concentrated. I could live-stream Occupy Wall Street protests and Skype with a colleague from Tokyo about graphic novels; I could do this on my iPhone while I'm in a park in Union Square, eating a local organic apple that I bought at the Farmer's market. We of course have a desire to connect, to make communities, and we've designed technology to do just that.

Now, does it give us more a sense of empathy? A deeper understanding of other cultures? Or is it flat-lining everything to digestive, consumerist bite-sized chunks? Neurologists talk about how all this multi-tasking of information has physically altered our brains so information doesn't seep in the same way that it used to. So does living in virtual hybrid worlds deeply affect our consciousness, change our moral behavior? Or do we become reduced to this Lacanian fantasy of pure gaze? Protests like Occupy Wall Street and seeing how fast it has virally spread to other countries, does give me hope.

EZW: Your approach to poetry is nonlinear. You create wandering forms and offer hybrid structures and vocabularies. Does poetry need to migrate in order to survive?

CPH: Yes, I do think that. Poetry has migrated for centuries. Our definition of what poetry has been redefined again and again. It was a scandal when we got rid of rhyme; it was a scandal when we got rid of meter; it was a scandal when we got rid of the line; and now what do we have left that we consider sacred for poetry? The page?

Of course, oration has been the original method of disseminating poetry but I'm curious to see how poetry will evolve as the book becomes more digital. Will we follow or fall behind? We can be radical by being resolute about poetry's obsolescence, by insisting on the materiality of the book but if that were to happen, wouldn't the poetry book become even more of an *object*, a *curio*, something to be almost fetishized, in the way we fetishize records? Would it become a souvenir, commodity as collector's item?

We can take advantage and reformulate what makes a poetry book; we can use the changing medium to awaken us to the endless possibilities of what poetry can be. We can project the poems in space, embed video, or use audio sound with text, or find alternative ways to perform poetry. Why, for instance, do we stick to this dull curriculum of readings (mike, podium, rows of metal chairs, it's all so dreary), the

> *"We can take advantage and reformulate what makes a poetry book; we can use the changing medium to awaken us to the endless possibilities of what poetry can be."*

academic conference, the panel of three or four poets taking turns reading from papers? Of course, there's performance poetry but it's so divided in a nonacademic/academic way. It would be exciting if there were mergers, offshoots, cross-breeding of performances. It wouldn't take much to shake it up.

EZW: Your poetry is a study of language and plays with colloquial and foreign structures. In *Dance Dance Revolution*, you actually invent a creole. Has your work ever been translated? Is the creole penetrable for non-English speakers?
CPH: I have a family friend who we call Uncle Kim whose English is impeccable, though he never even spent any time in the States. He's wicked brilliant and he has a penchant for interesting headware like a doo rag with a marijuana leaf on it. After he read my book, he said, "Uncle Kim's English is no good. My English is too ESL for your book. But I will study hard so that I can understand your poems!"

      If someone like Uncle Kim can barely understand it, then I don't know about non-English speakers. But I have had a few Spanish friends who were enticed by the book because of the Spanish and other language usages. No one has tried to translate *Dance Dance Revolution*. I'm not sure if it's possible. There was a Pen World Translation Slam and a German poet was going to translate from it but he chose a poem that wasn't in creole.

EZW: Do you tend to enjoy reading translations of poetry?
CPH: Some of my favorite collections are translations – such as Inger Christensen's *Alphabet*. And though Paul Celan is notoriously difficult to translate, I still fell in love with the force of his poems from Michael Hamburger's and John Felstiner's translations.

      Of course, there are poems where I feel the music in translations is not coming across, where it feels muted, and wish I could read the original. I feel that way about the Russian poets, especially Osip Mandelstam, and many translations of Asian poets. Most Korean translations, with the exception of a few like translator and poet Don Mee Choi's translations, are terrible because not enough poets translate Korean poets.

EZW: Have you traveled much? How important is it for a writer to be well traveled?
CPH: I love traveling and don't travel nearly enough. I feel both a sense of calm and exhilaration when I'm elsewhere. My dream career is Anthony Bourdain's job. I would like to have a camera follow me around as I wander food stalls in Singapore, trying different versions of chicken rice, or go on a wild boar hunt in New Zealand. But obviously it's not necessary. Look at Dickinson.

as I remember the details what proof in Alaska

you died near Willow, beyond Wasilla
almost in sight of Denali
at the funeral home I got inside the oven
where they would burn you
saw its ceramic insides
the gaps of light shining between
material bricks, felt its warmth
heard the high whine
industrial strength engine firing up
the furnace coming on
the power it took
to incinerate you
my darling

I wonder which way up
your poor mangled body lay
inside the measly
pauper's cardboard box

I stood over you
my hands pressing down
into you to know that in reality
you were dead inside,
about to be burnt,
that you would stay dead

the undertaker in his dark suit
tried to stop me
perhaps unused to such
maternal determination or
insubordination
this is my child I said
he shut up after that

my two sons, husband,
her best friends stood looking on,
the undertakers' smell of cheap
rancid powdered vanilla
like a brothel lavatory I imagine
there were plastic flowers
everywhere &
they gave me a plastic fan

with a photo of their
establishment & services listed
in case I ever needed them again
I didn't need them then

cleanser, deodorizer, room
freshener? or sickly scented candles
I would prefer
to smell burning bodies
than that smell ever again
I do not know if I said anything
there was nothing to say

as I remember
as I recall
the unimaginable

what you'd expect in Sarah Palin territory
I think the next big town was Wasilla

break up

the loons are exchanging their mournful
haunting cries to each other across the lake
oh no that's not quite accurate
breakup's a few weeks off yet

there are days I'm tempted
to pretend you are taking a day off
from the clinic
days I pretend to see you
bent down gardening & blissful
up to the elbows in earth, concocting meals
& curries from scratch with your mate.
It's may, near your birthday,
& your favorite freesias have
almost come up, the poppies,
your blue irises & you are
lost in joy on this almost spring
Alaska day of my imagining

we know we're playing with fire & ice
when we decide to, gingerly, step across
the frozen but thawing in places ice,
arms about each other's waists
taking a risk of its holding us up
like times in childhood when parents
had expressly forbidden it
& we defied them

you, feather-light, even well-bundled up
ruddy-cheeked your nose sharp as a pen
my fingers waxy yellow as the dead
my Raynaud's syndrome kicking in
sliding feet shuffling forward
as if we were wearing sloppy bedroom slippers
to test each step on the ice, crazing
but both of us knowing quite well
what ice we were skating on
knowing the consequences would be freezing
hell if we fell through into black water

two adults who knew better
knew how dangerous it was

hell you were a nurse practitioner
non-conformist (though you had a streak
of the fire & the wild in you too)

but oh the lure of the lake

the sparkle & crackle of sunlight
on snow ice dazzle & the giggles & slips
& silliness of us mittened mother & daughter
nose tips & cheeks ruddy
sharing an adventure
that only one of us will be left to remember

we had to shuffle swift a little
as if we had bound feet
so as not to rest our weight for too long
in any given place

a glissade our scurrying slide
the crisp air, the subterranean ominous
sound of ice splintering, crackling,
giving way just behind us & beneath
a blue sound, without pigment

just as sudden & swift as in the end you left
us bereft like the forsaken merman
teaching me then not to think
any of us is safe no matter what or where
we weigh our weight we're all skating

                                        over thin ice

PHO

Sometimes you can't be cheered up. My grandfather once told me
don't order seafood at a steak restaurant.
Today after work I wanted a burrito. Walked to the corner
burritoria, it was freezing and the truck was gone.

Kennan was cranky, she wanted pho. I caved. I hadn't in six,
seven years had pho. My Republican friend Bob
once tricked me into ordering tripe. It was disgusting.
We crossed the gas station parking lot,

passed the Ukrainian deli and family pizzeria
into Un-Pho-Gettable. One woman
was in the restaurant with the small
Vietnamese lady behind the counter.

I'd like to go to Vietnam. The other woman
was in a cutoff brewpub hoodie, her nails long as pulltabs,
we didn't talk much. Kennan ordered chicken pho.
I was firm, got the tofu yakisoba.

The order came– hers lovingly separated into soup, noodles,
cut peppers, and siracha with plum sauce
cocktail on the side. The yakisoba–– a tangle of bland
yellow in styrofoam.

Only three chunks of tofu. I hate wasting
money on dinner as need, not energy, not delight. Sadly,
this was the second time I've had to settle
for something else. I'm worried

about my inability to get a burrito after a long day of work,
a quick fix, I don't have the energy to eat other shit.
The White Stripes were on the radio
coming into the city. I had been happy,

now I was a settled-for dinner. A beer
didn't help. My grandfather is long gone. I wish
I'd never been tricked into eating tripe, I wish Pop
wasn't dead. I worry about burritos, I worry

the truck won't come back, I worry about our relationship,
how only one of us can be happy at a time.

AND IF I HAD A DAUGHTER, I'D NAME HER LILLE

Got off the train in Paris. Late. Gare Du Nord looked like the Monet painting it was, wet and gray and tons of shades of black. Athena and I were lost. We had to walk. We had big backpacker backpacks and set out across the city. We had to piss. Like ugly Americans we stopped in McDonalds– where else can you go without someone asking questions? My ankles were killing me. Fuck that backpacking around Europe. Took a train to some city, hoped it'd be cheaper than Paris. It was. We got a hotel room for a few nights– we were broke, broke, broke. Fucked a lot and ate kebab sandwiches from the La Pyramid taco truck thing– just like LA really, but colder and somehow romantic. I really don't remember what else happened in Lille, but there were some days. My ankles, really my Achilles tendon, started bothering me today– in the graveyard with Kennan. It was a wet spring in Seattle, a lot like Paris. She asked me two weeks ago about marriage. I want to talk about children. At Pere Lachaise we split a ham sandwich and walked the city of the dead. It was beautiful. The cemetery in Seattle is hilly. It dips at one point into a hollow and the headstones are circling round and round like rings, or mixing bowls of something, and at the deepest part is a reflecting pool, a brass bird and two trees and it is beautiful– like connecting two worlds.

LAST STOP

The doughty Foster Freeze at the foot of University where cars
exit from 80 after the long trip cross-country was built in the 50s

and now inhabits memory like the senile card shark wandering
the halls of the old folks home; he was once the life of the party,

turning jazz clubs and hotel lobbies into a momentary beltway
to the stars, but now reaches for the belt of withered ladies until

they snap the way the stressed mom snaps because Dad keeps
pushing until presto, a new world is born—your young eyes in

the back seat softened by the promise of ice cream and a brand
new town because your father's instinct to rebuild in the land of

everything's possible slides from his fears like a prick from its
sheath until you are left with only the taste of this sweet cream

and a last leg of street deep into the westering dream; the hoary
window slides open when you near it and out comes the dark

arm with the squat waffle cone, its glamorous top as white as the
stark way we talk when people land juiced on flowers because

this peaceful finish is not finished at all but a long spit of sand
that stretches into the sea-born storm—body after body testing

the sly wind like the old mother-ache in the woman who knows
why her man is coming and how a young boy can sharpen his

happiness by taking pleasure in old habits and familiar names
as if the instinct to build thrills out of nothing much was new.

KENT

Time is the great entertainer, he said, gazing out over the corn at the border
of two Midwestern states; the year was 1969 and the way his sandals took

paths, slipping into the depressions like gel, rolling over the hillocks as
easy as his massive Olds did roads—as soft as fresh fur contours the body,

especially if yours…somehow mirrored the state we were in—two states:
machines dragged into the den to have their way with us, and then of course

the primitive: this corn, a breakfast slab of bacon and leeks, and the plants
we ingested afterwards that made it all so unique—everything was up for

reinterpretation, including the tools in the barn, the musty leather straps,
the rusting iron; they could just as easily have been put there to trigger our

collective memory, without which we rot like fruit after great emancipating
storms; more for us than men who two hundred years ago broke the news

of these fertile plains; Kent slept in the barn, pulled fat tomatoes from the
vines that had crawled away from packaging like teens in sudden love and

that time in particular—of unwise war—was defined by acts, courageous
provocateurs atop the flagpoles waving another flag, paddling from cities

in beechbark canoes, which is why Kent kept his Bible in the barn, along
with Gurdjieff, Yeats…boots for wading into the hay that smelled like mask;

the time blew with bells on, with sparks from the squawk box, with what
we were becoming—our own special brand that swarmed with riled insects,

and the damage drugs would do…the dark afterglow of the carnal ride;
time was the anvil and the anvil's sound, then the shoe itself leaking beast;

it was the way we sat on the porch listening to the fall come, the day we
ran up rows in the fields, let ponds make whoopee with our wired bodies

as they threaded the here and now; even the castile soap he squirted into
the claw-footed tub wormed the Greek out of the sweet nymphets modeling

on the bottle, which created the smell of a long yesteryear, and promised
wild atavistic times to come. It's a carnival, Kent said, I'm glad to be alive.

SAILOR

Halyards clink on the marina's winter forest
of aluminum masts. *Jasmine* tugs at her dock lines,
sighs against her fenders. Her 36' decks are faded,

lines worn, Lifesling not checked in years.
Within her locked cabin, the old master's guidebooks, logs,
splicing tools are stowed away. With the master,

a jazz pianist when ashore, she could journey
the world. For six years since his passing, the master's wife
steers *Jasmine* to nearby summer dependables—

Rosario Strait, Sucia Island, Spencer Spit. Despite her firm gaze,
the wife is unsure. Each season she ponders,
Is it time to sell?

Friends and a new man or two have come aboard,
but the widow remains alone, dependent on a local boat service
to *take care of everything*.

Freezing rain slants across the harbor, finds its way
over the breakwater. Fingers of ice grip
Jasmine's wheel. She shudders in her slip.

TRAILER

He steps off twelve paces, confirms
the rotting hulk, buried by alder and cedar, is a 35-footer
like the one he lived in with his mother
and stepfather. He sets aside bird watching, tucks binoculars
under his shoulder, steps into a pungent realm
of rotting laminates, moldy curtains.

Enough remains—
here the tiny bathroom, there the kitchen,
the foldout dining table.
At the front was a hideaway bed, all the room
he had to himself. He folded and put away
bedding each morning, though he could leave
his army men, cigar box of treasures, some books
on the window shelf. At the foot of the bed
he once nursed his black mutt, Hey You,
after she swallowed a chicken bone.

The far end was unknown, forbidden—*their place*.
Fifty years later he peers into the tatters
of a stranger's bedroom, feels the mystery
of his mother and Dick's presence, hears
the nightly cries of loving and hating
he could not escape.

A Wilson's Warbler sings
from nearby willows.
Shaking his head, the man steps out of shadows,
focuses on the bit of yellow-feathered
life that calls him
back into spring.

FATHER

Me almost not turning back
and then turning back
as the welding torch
set you on fire.

The way you said my name
as if you were very sick
the way you beat out the flames
before I had to decide.

BEDTIME STORY

God is done for the day.
The kids are kissed and tucked in.
He's in the john
brushing his teeth
and taking off his shirt,
listening to their tiny breath
and thinking the moon,
as it throws its light
on the shower curtain,
was a good job of it.

As each button opens
the night gets a little
darker. God's silver head
in the silver mirror above
the sink glows like the moon
and he turns on a river
of water that is in a hurry
to be elsewhere. He troubles its flow
with rock-hard hands.
A trout takes shelter
under his thumb
and God watches and waits, knowing
he has painted a fine and ticklish line
of desire inside every creature,
that it will move on,
and it moves on.

A slight noise comes from the yard
as a mountain lion catches
a four-point buck. God
pauses to make sure the cat
doesn't want to come in,
and rolls his undershirt over his head.
The cat does not want to come in.

TOOTHBRUSH

For a man who barely ate
he sure brushed his teeth a lot.
After his son found the painter's body,
it was lifted from the upstairs bedroom
twelve paces from his son's, where
we'd made love all year without
caution, knowing the old man
removed his hearing aid whenever
alone or hoping to be left alone,
when the sounds of the surface
world swelled to a high pitched ringing,
violins tuning endlessly in a hollow
hall, insects whining above
the tight skin of a lake, and also
knowing that if he did, the faint
music of our departure and arrival
would likely give him purpose
in the studio that afternoon
where he'd add marigold and ochre
to the thick rose of a woman's cheek.
The single letter to whom it may concern,
detailing the ways his death would not
be described, revising the portrait
we'd all paint under his brush,
editing his exit down
to short fiction, was not enough
to cover the young son and the grown
son, the adopted Indian daughter, his assistant
Tracy, the grandkids, the biographers
and their books, complete but for
the final chapter. His young son
stiff, too, but searching, tortured the house
to find his own goodbye, a small envelope
somewhere on a stool in the custard yellow
studio, under a hard cold mattress,
in an underwear drawer, a deep breast
pocket, where at least he'd held it close.
And although we'd witnessed
the fierce green core of his selfishness,
his grief a porous chunk of pumice
never a means to polish ivory,
but carried by water, ill with holes,

we held on to hope that he'd left
more than a damp toothbrush
on the kitchen counter, flecks of carrot
lodged in the thick baleen of bristles,
suddenly useless in the afterlife.

EXITS

Seldom marked by grace. Deep in the warren,
a doe kindles her kits. Altricial statements of thin bone,
weak with mammalian want. To enter this world
as a thing of prey. To know last not
as survival, as fit lingering, but birth
the first ticking. Mean means
to an end. Say lasting
impossible. Say it will be,
but it won't be long.
Deliver in dirt.
Fear the badger,
Iberian lynx, red fox.
Taste the salted
risk of afterbirth.
When an odd rib
rakes the burrow,
save time, feast
straight from
the nest.

chapter 5 第五回: the spirit of lin daiyu's daughter visits a red temple, goldfish swim beneath Buddha's feet, a woman in jeans and Converse composes verses caught from falling flowers

sandalwood smoke in remembrance of
        the one who burned
        the one who drowned
        and another
        in remembrance of the child not born
        the child still born
        and another

As I descend the wet stone staircase, an old woman limps up the base
of the mountain with a black gun in her hand. She is pointing it at her head.
There is a click, then a laugh. The gun is fake. She keeps walking. I am
    walking toward her.
The young boy asks what she is doing. I say:
    She's mentally ill. She doesn't know what she is doing.

She keeps limping along, gun pointed at her right temple, pulling the trigger,
    laughing,
pulling the trigger. Bright pink petals on her rayon pants flutter in the white
    wind.

The old woman continues up the hill toward the temple as I continue down
    the stone
steps. I reach the dirt path that leads through a tunnel of trees to the parking
    lot. At the
edge of the pavement, a woman stands beside her red motorbike, selling the
    sweet beancurd
she has made by hand. Into the mist above the trees of Qingchengshan,
rises her voice from the loudspeaker:

豆腐花   豆腐花   豆腐花

WARRIOR POSE

arms   stretched   outward

left knee bent, right leg
extended, foot turned in
she turns her head to
focus on her left hand
stops   before she gets
there   on the pile
of bricks in the corner
a dead cricket's body lies

m m e r ing   in morning's
 i   fifth
 h   golden
s   light

how long has he been there

why hasn't anyone noticed

a note suspended   sings down mulberry leaf veins
green-yellow passages from   this
   Peking Opera song she cannot name

a teacher's voice grows distant

she bends her knee deeper, focus focus,   but the cricket is   still there
  and what if someone picks up the brick and doesn't see him

in the third breath   she cannot stay
  she walks to the corner, kneels beside bricks

a cricket's body disintegrates into steel gray
flakes of graphite fallen to form a pool

   beside the rest of the body   still there

      how long has he been here

  the old man still sings   passages
   from a Perking opera   in the shade of the wooden pavilion
  where animals once lay   sacrificed to gods
  the well, now cemented over, supports the weight of the man's feet

  a teacher counts backwards

    十   九   八

sunlight   七   on roof-tiles 六 makes the 五

pavilion 四 appear 三 wet

     二   一

   when she lifts the brick the cricket's thin-line-legs
    catch the wind and begin to move, and for a moment
   she thinks maybe he is still alive but injured
    but the steel-gray dust of the missing part of his body
   tells her no.   she looks into the yellow-white sky
   not knowing where to take him.

all around her students straighten their legs,
   inhale to prepare for the other side

where do the dead go
where do the dead go,
   magpie in the mulberry,
     where do the dead go

CONTRIBUTORS

Tory Adkisson was born in West Covina, raised in the High Desert, and currently lives in Columbus, Ohio, where he is an MFA candidate at The Ohio State University. He also serves as poetry editor of *The Journal*. His poems have appeared or are forthcoming in *CutBank, West Branch Wired, Hayden's Ferry Review, Quarterly West, Cream City Review, Salamander, Cave Wall,* and *Third Coast*, among others. He is currently applying to PhD programs and working on his first collection.

Dan Alter has poems recently published in *Saint Anne's Review, Poetica, Assembly, Prime Number,* and *Zeek*. He was a finalist for the 2008-2009 Anna Davidson Rosenberg Awards for Poems on the Jewish Experience. In 1992 he was an Arad Arts Project Fellow. He lives in Berkeley, California with his wife Jess and daughter Hadas, where he makes his living as an electrician.

Brent Armendinger is the author of two chapbooks of poetry: *Undetectable* (Diagram/New Michigan Press) and *Archipelago* (Noemi Press). His work has recently appeared in *Court Green, LIT, Puerto del Sol,* and *Volt*. He teaches creative writing and literature at Pitzer College in Claremont, CA.

Jia Oak Baker is originally from Los Angeles, California. She received a BA in English from Brigham Young University, a MEd from Arizona State University, and is pursuing a MFA in Writing and Literature at Bennington College where she is a recipient of a Liam Rector Scholarship. Her poetry is forthcoming in *Thin Air Magazine*.

Joan Baranow is an Associate Professor of English at Dominican University of California. Her poetry has appeared in *The Paris Review, Western Humanities Review, The Antioch Review, The Western Journal of Medicine,* and other magazines. Her book of poetry, *Living Apart*, was published by Plain View Press. With her husband, SVCW poet David Watts, she produced the PBS documentary *Healing Words: Poetry & Medicine*.

Lucy Diamond Biederman lives in Fairfax, Virginia, where she attended George Mason University's MFA program in creative writing. Her poems have appeared in *No Tell Motel, Gargoyle, Smartish Pace, The Journal, The Cimarron Review,* and other journals. Her chapbook, *The Other World*, is forthcoming from dancing girl press in May 2012.

Teresa Breeden is confounded by the naming of things. Her words attempt to express what's inside of titles. To un-name and reorganize. To discover what is already known, like returning home after a long journey. Though well-traveled, Teresa's favorite landscape is the high desert of her Nevada hometown in the Sierra foothills. Recent publications include the traveling art show "Always Lost; A Meditation on War," *Best New Poets 2010*, and *Mamas and Papas* (Anthology).

Joe Cadora's stories have appeared in various literary periodicals including *Southern Humanities Review* and the *Montserrat Review*, whose editors nominated him for the Pushcart Prize. His reviews of literary fiction have appeared in the *San Francisco Chronicle*. His literary awards include the Eisner Prize, the Fabilli-Hoffer Essay Prize, the Julia Shrout Short Story Prize, the Stronach Prize for both prose and poetry, and the Elizabeth Crothers Prize. His translation of Rainer Maria Rilke's *New Poems* will be published in Spring 2013 by Copper Canyon Press.

Brent Calderwood's poems have appeared in *American Poetry Journal, Poets & Artists, Crab Creek Review, The Gay & Lesbian Review Worldwide,* and *The Southern Poetry Anthology*; his poem "The Golden Hour" was chosen by Mark Doty as winner of the 2011 AQLF Broadside Contest. He is the Literary Editor for *A&U Magazine* and Associate Editor for Lambda Literary and the poetry journal *Assaracus.*

Elizabeth Chapman's poems have appeared in journals including *Sand Hill Review, Water-Stone Review, Poetry, Cider Press Review,* and *Rattle.* Her chapbook, *Creekwalker*, was published by (M)other Tongue Press (1995). She has seen two full-length collections into print: *Candlefish* (University of Arkansas Press, 2004) and *Light Thickens* (Ashland Poetry Press, 2009). The latter was awarded the Robert McGovern Publication Prize for poetry. Previously a college teacher of English literature, and, for twenty years, a psychotherapist in private practice, she lives and works in Palo Alto, California.

Brian Cochran lives and writes in St Louis, Missouri, often simultaneously.

Chris Cummings. Bio/confession: I've been writing poetry since the 6th grade. I got an MFA from Bennington a few years ago. I'm frequently distracted from poetry by other loves (cooking, gardening with native plants being the two most frequent distractors) but these loves seem to feed each other. A few years ago, something inside told me to lend my voice to the voiceless nonhuman world and I try to do that in poems; some of these have been published. Squaw this summer opened my eyes to a whole new way of working. Hope to see you all again at future SVCW poetry camps.

David Cummings. What's to say? I write lots of unpublished poems, since the late '70s. (Like the song says, "You've [as in poems] gotten to be a habit with me.") A few published here and there; a few near misses in the endless round of chapbook and manuscript contests. (Do not think of the hamster, the wire wheel, the cage!) But on a lighter note, I've been to SVCW poetry workshops some half-dozen times, and the experience has always been absolutely fabulous. Just poetry! Hoping to be back in two years; hoping to see old friends again.

Austin Ellis is an MFA student at UCI.

Ken Haas was born in New York City, went to college in the Boston area and attended graduate school in England. He now lives in San Francisco, where he works in biotechnology, and also has a home in Truckee. His work has appeared or is forthcoming in *Caesura, Hawai'i Pacific Review, Chest Journal, The Squaw Valley Review, Tattoo Highway, Natural Bridge,* the Sixteen Rivers Press anthology *The Place That Inhabits Us,* etc.

Marcelo Hernandez Castillo was born in Zacatecas, Mexico and raised in Yuba City, California. He studied creative writing at California State University Sacramento where he earned his BA in English Literature. He served as poetry section editor for *Calaveras Station Literary Journal* and, with Robert Hass, edited the *Squaw Valley Review 2011.* He was a Bazzannela Literary Award winner for 2010 and has received scholarships from the Warmdal and Willhelm Memorial Scholarship fund and the Squaw Valley Community of Writers. His work appears in *Carcinogenic Poetry, The Legendary, Sex and Murder Magazine, Softblow Review, Puffin Circus, Psychic Meatloaf, Calaveras Station,* and *Somos en Escritos* among others. He was accepted into the University of Michigan's MFA in poetry where he will begin his graduate studies in the fall of 2012. He currently works as a handyman and is recently married.

Brenda Hillman is the author of eight collections of poetry, all published by Wesleyan University Press, the most recent of which are *Cascadia* (2001) and *Pieces of Air in the Epic* (2005), which received the William Carlos Williams Prize for Poetry, and *Practical Water* (2009). She has also published three chapbooks. With Patricia Dienstfrey, she edited *The Grand Permission: New Writings on Poetics and Motherhood* (Wesleyan, 2003). Hillman teaches at St. Mary's College where she is the Olivia Filippi Professor of Poetry; she works with CodePink, a social justice group against war and lives in the San Francisco Bay Area.

Amy Hoffmann is a third generation California native. She has a BA in English and Journalism from the University of Southern California and currently writes poetry, teaches Pilates, and moonlights as a clown. She has been published in *The Great American Poetry Show* and *Calyx.* She is a founding member of the San Francisco Women's Poetry Collective and leads writing workshops in Half Moon Bay where she lives in a cottage by a creek with her husband Tom, daughter Poppy, and cat Snoop.

RJ Ingram is graduating with a BFA in creative writing from Bowling Green State University in spring 2012. He serves as the poetry editor of *Prairie Margins* and as an associate poetry editor of *Mid American Review.* His most recent publications can be found in *Revolution House, Alice Blue Review,* and *Spittoon.*

Bonnie S. Kaplan, a native of Los Angeles, has been a featured writer with Valley Contemporary Poets (2010) and contributed to the anthology *Mentsh: On Being Queer and Jewish* (2004). She holds an MFA in Performance Art from the California College of Arts and Crafts and for the past decade has worked as a teacher in the California Corrections system, helping prepare parolees to re-enter the community. She is grateful to the Squaw Valley Writer's Workshop and is still learning not to run with the bat.

Gary Leising is the author of the chapbook *Fastened to a Dying Animal*, available from Pudding House Publications. His poems have appeared in journals including *Waccamaw, River Styx, Poemeleon, The Cincinnati Review*, and elsewhere. He lives in Utica, New York, where he is associate professor of English at Utica College.

Bonnie Long gave away her management books and began writing poetry when she retired. Her poems have received awards in the annual Jessamyn West Creative Writing Contest in the Napa Valley and appear in the 2010 and 2011 Marin Poetry Center Annual Anthologies and June 2011 issue of *Spillway*. She lives in St. Helena, CA, where she serves as a trustee on the library board.

Terry Lowe composed her first poem at the age of four (lovingly preserved by her mother) and kept at it all the way through college. She then chose to pursue graduate studies in philosophy—thinking that a more practical path than poetry—and, for more years than she likes to admit, forgot how much she loves writing poems. Happily, poetry did not forget her, and her work has now appeared in the *Naugatuck River Review* and the online journal of the Nevada County Women's Writing Salon. She lives in the San Francisco Bay Area, to which she returned in 2012 after 11 years of residence in Rough and Ready, California.

Sally Allen McNall has written and taught in Oregon, Arizona, Kansas, New Zealand, Ohio, and California. She began publishing poems in 1985, when her youngest child left home, and has published steadily since then in a wide variety of journals and magazines, off and online. Her chapbook, *How to Behave at the Zoo and Other Lessons*, was a winner of the State Street Press competition in 1997, and her first book manuscript, *Rescue*, won the Backwaters Press Prize in 1999. A chapbook, *Trying to write a poem without the word blood in it*, came out in 2005 from PWJ Publishing. A second book, *Where Once*, is 2010 Editor's Choice from Main Street Rag, mostly elegies for the natural world.

Steve Rempe was born in Marin County, California. Currently living in Novato, CA, married with two adult children and one granddaughter. Owner of a green building certified construction company for over 32 years, active in the community supporting the Youth Center, other community organizations such as school music and arts programs, civic planning groups, and some arts and family organizations outside the Bay Area. Time off is spent with family, listening to and playing music, writing, traveling.

When he was 14 years old, **Larry Ruth** set out from Yosemite Valley with a friend and together they hiked the John Muir Trail. They spent the last night on Mount Whitney in a snowstorm in July. Larry is now a consultant in natural resource and environmental policy. He has also served as a board member for environmental nonprofit organizations. For many years he conducted research and handled programmatic responsibilities at the University of California, Berkeley. He taught courses in environmental policy and law. Publications include articles on federal wildland fire policy, ecosystem sustainability, forest policy in the Sierra Nevada, and adaptive management.

gini savage has written several books including *Gripe Water*. Her CD Cherries & her poetry cycle Natural Selection, with original music by Jake Heggie, are frequently performed. She is currently working on a chapbook about her beloved only daughter Jess who died in 2007. gini spends weekends napping in Napa with her husband Michael & dog Nero & weekdays dabbling at the yoga center she has run for 28 years with her partner Suzanne. Poetry, opera & acting fill in any other gaps.

Catharine Clark-Sayles practices medicine in the San Francisco area. She has had poems published in numerous medical journals and anthologies including the recent *The Place That Inhabits Us* and *The Healing Art of Writing*. Her first book of poems, *One Breath*, was published by Tebot Bach Press in 2008. Her second book, *Lifeboat,* will be published this year. She has attended the Squaw Valley Community of Writers in 2009 and 2011.

Brent Schaeffer was born and raised in Eagle River, Alaska. His poetry has appeared in *Green Mountains Review, Poet Lore, New Mexico Poetry Review, the Peninsula Clarion,* and *Rivets.* His interview with Simon Armitage is forthcoming in *Willow Springs.* He has taught writing in the East Bay Area of California and around the Northwest. He lives in Seattle and loves the Philadelphia Eagles.

Eliot Schain's work has been published in *Ploughshares* and *American Poetry Review*, among others, and is included in two recent anthologies: *The Place That Inhabits Us: Poems of the San Francisco Bay Watershed* and *Bear Flag Republic: Prose Poems and Poetics from California.* His collection, *Westering Angels*, is available from Zeitgeist Press. Additional poems can be found at his website: eliotschain. com.

David Stallings was born in the U.S. South, raised in Alaska and Colorado before settling in the Pacific Northwest. Once an academic geographer, he has spent many years promoting public transportation in the Puget Sound area. His poems have appeared in several North American and UK literary journals and anthologies.

Chris Wilson's poems have appeared in *Fourteen Hills* and the *Tupelo Press Poetry Project*. Wilson is a graduate student at San Francisco State University and Pacific Lutheran University.

Erica Zora Wrightson is a Pasadena native who writes about proximities, distances, and the ingredients of place. She is a writer/editor for the Museum of Contemporary Art, Los Angeles, and lives in Angeleno Heights.

Jami Proctor-Xu is a poet, translator, scholar, and mother. She grew up in Tucson and currently lives in Beijing. She writes in Chinese and English. Her poems, essays, and translations have appeared in journals in the U.S. and China such as *Chinese Literature Today, Switchback, Du Shi, Qinghai Lake International Poetry Festival Special Issue*, and *Shi Lin*.